Wally Amos

and his famous cookies

by Jeri Cipriano

Boston, Massachusetts
Chandler, Arizona
Glenview, Illinois
Upper Saddle River, New Jersey

Illustrations
2, 3, 5, 6, 8, 9, 11, 12, 14 Roger Stewart.

Photographs
Every effort has been made to secure permission and provide appropriate credit for photographic material.
The publisher deeply regrets any omission and pledges to correct errors called to its attention in subsequent editions.

Unless otherwise acknowledged, all photographs are the property of Pearson Education, Inc.

Photo locators denoted as follows: Top (T), Center (C), Bottom (B), Left (L), Right (R), Background (Bkgd)

4 Comstock Images/Thinkstock; 7 Library of Congress; 10 kgelster/iStockphoto; 15 Dana Edmunds, courtesy of Wally Amos.

ISBN-13: 978-0-328-67621-7
ISBN-10: 0-328-67621-7

10 11 12 V0SI 18 17 16 15

The "People Business"

For most of his life, Wally Amos looked for ways to make money. He wanted to support himself and his family. In the 1970s, he thought up his best business idea yet. He created a company called Famous Amos Chocolate Chip Cookies.

People everywhere gobbled up the cookies. What was the secret ingredient? Some would say it was Amos himself. He liked people, and they liked him. The people Amos met didn't usually forget him. "I am in the people business, not the cookie business," he once said. This is the story of how one person created a world-famous cookie.

Wally as a young boy

Wally Amos was born July 1, 1936, in Tallahassee, Florida. His mother, Ruby, cleaned people's houses. His father, Wallace, worked for a gas company. Both of his parents worked hard at their jobs. They taught Amos to work hard at whatever he did.

Amos also learned about good manners from his parents. He said things like "Yes, sir" and "No, ma'am." He respected adults. Good manners helped Amos in business when he got older.

A Young Businessman

As a child, Amos wanted to make his own money. He started a shoeshine business. He cleaned people's shoes. He had a **reputation** for being the best shoe shiner around.

Young Amos wanted to make more money, so he got another job. He began delivering newspapers to people's homes. At first he delivered them on foot, but it was hard. His parents got him a bicycle, which made his work easier. Amos worked hard at this job. He was one of the best newspaper boys.

A shoeshine box

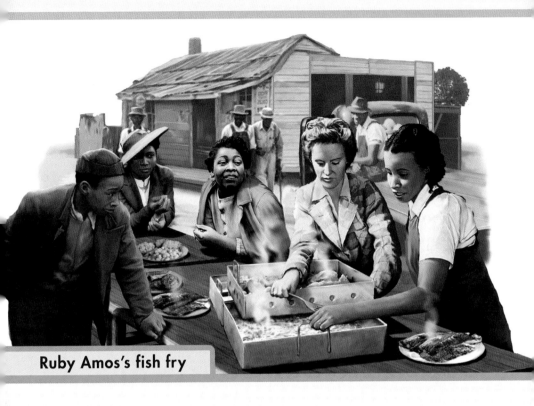

Ruby Amos's fish fry

Amos also had a third job helping his mother. Every week Ruby Amos held a Friday night fish fry. She served fish, chicken, and side dishes. Almost everyone in the community came to eat there. They talked with their friends and paid to eat the tasty food.

Amos delivered food to people who couldn't make it down to the fish fry. He was always polite to his customers and chatted with them. Customers liked Amos and gave him **tips**. His parents' lessons about good manners had paid off.

Separate Schools

When he wasn't working, Amos was going to school. Every day he walked miles to and from school. Amos went to a school for African American children even though there was a school closer to his home. During this time in the South, black children and white children were not allowed to go to the same school.

Amos saw that white children had better schools. He thought this was unfair. But his mother taught Amos another valuable lesson—to hold his head high and believe in himself.

New York, New York

Amos's parents divorced when he was twelve. At first he and his mother moved to Orlando, Florida. Then his mother decided to send him to New York City to live with his Aunt Della. Ruby Amos believed that there were better opportunities for African Americans in New York.

Amos liked the big city. He was fascinated by the tall buildings and subways. He especially loved living with his aunt. She made the best chocolate chip cookies he had ever tasted. Della taught him how to make them. Amos had no idea then how much Aunt Della's chocolate chip cookies would affect his life.

New York City

Amos during his
Air Force days

Amos worked lots of different jobs when he lived in New York City. He delivered newspapers and groceries. He also went to a school that trained students to become chefs. Amos quit the school when he learned that he was not being given the same job training opportunities that white students were given.

Over the next few years, Amos tried different things. He joined the Air Force. Then he got a job at a clothing store. As usual, he worked hard at everything he did.

Show Business

When he was in his 20s, Amos got married and had children. He needed money to support his family, so he got a job at a talent company. The company helped find work for people in show business, such as musicians and actors. Amos first worked in the mailroom. During his breaks, he did odd jobs around the office. His bosses liked that he worked hard and gave him better paying jobs. Soon he was working as an **agent**.

As an agent, Amos worked with many famous musicians, such as the female singing group the Supremes. He was good at his job. In 1967, Amos moved to Los Angeles, California. He started his own talent company.

The Supremes

In Los Angeles, Amos struggled to get his company off the ground. He couldn't always pay his bills. He started to grow tired of show business.

Whenever he felt bad, Amos baked cookies. This reminded him of the good times he had with Aunt Della. Amos realized his true passion was baking cookies. He wondered if he could create a business based on them.

The Cookie King

Amos needed money to start a business. He asked some of his famous friends from show business for help. They gave him $25,000.

In March 1975, Amos opened the Famous Amos Chocolate Chip Cookie store in Los Angeles. He gave both his name and his face to the company. A picture of Amos wearing a white hat and white shirt was on every bag of cookies that he sold.

Amos worked day and night. Customers loved the cookies. They told their friends and the Famous Amos name grew.

Amos's store was successful right away. Within a few months, he opened a second store. By the end of the first year, company sales reached $300,000.

Amos did a lot to **promote** his chocolate chip cookies. Soon he really was famous. He did magazine interviews, made television commercials, and even appeared in the Macy's Thanksgiving Day Parade. Company sales kept increasing, too. By 1982, sales reached $12 million.

Amos in the Macy's Thanksgiving Day Parade in 1980

By the mid-1980s, everyone in the country knew who Amos was. However, just as Amos seemed to be at his most successful, his business began to fall apart. Amos was great at promoting the cookies, but he did not know much about running the day-to-day business of a huge company. The company was losing money. In the late 1980s, he sold the Famous Amos name and business to another company.

A Comeback

Amos did not let failure stop him. In the 1990s, he created a new company. This one sold fat-free muffins.

Then in 1998, the Keebler Company bought the Famous Amos Chocolate Chip Cookie Company. They asked Amos to come back and promote the cookies. Over the years the cookie recipe had been changed. The cookies didn't taste as good as they had before. Amos asked Keebler to change the recipe. They agreed. Soon Amos was back selling the delicious cookies based on Aunt Della's recipe.

As Amos grew older, he developed new interests. He wrote books and gave money to charities. In the early 2000s, he started an organization that encourages parents to read to their children every day.

Today, Wally Amos is known for his tasty cookies and a "can-do" attitude. He thinks it is important to have a belief in oneself in order to succeed. In one of his books, he leaves readers with this message: "If it could happen to me, Wally Amos. . . then it can happen to you."

Glossary

agent a person who represents another person in business

promote to help a business become better known

reputation the opinion people have of someone or something

tips small sums of money given for a service